Vulnerability in Silhouette
Poems

Vulnerability in Silhouette
Poems

T. L. Cooper

Copyright © 2015 T. L. Cooper
All rights reserved. Published in the United States by The TLC Press.

ISBN: 1943736006
ISBN-13: 978-1-943736-00-3

DEDICATION

Dedicated to all those who find
strength and courage in vulnerability.

Vulnerability

I show you me
Only a tiny glimpse
In hopes you'll see my truth
When you're receptive to a glimpse
I reveal a little more of me
Giving you enough
To keep you enticed
I don't wish to overwhelm you
Nor to tease you
I only want you to see me
As I truly am
And to love me as such
But I fear the vulnerability
That comes with the revelation of me
So I hold back little pieces
I hide my most sensitive vulnerabilities
I allow you a glimpse
Then I pull away
It is instinct
It is self-preservation
It is fear
I tell myself
Tomorrow I will risk showing you all of me
Knowing that tomorrow
I will convince myself you're not ready yet
When in reality
It is I who isn't strong enough to risk vulnerability
How long will you take the fragments I offer
Before you grow exasperated
Then the result will be the same
You'll be gone

And it'll be because I didn't have the strength
To tell you the truth of my heart
My silence will leave you blame free
At least if I tell you and you leave
I'll know it wasn't because I lacked courage
So I promise myself once again
Tomorrow I will be strong enough to risk
Vulnerability

A Slash, A Gash

Your words
Slashed a gash
Too deep for stitches
Into my being
Forcing me to see myself
In a whole new light
As my core bled through
Revealing all I'd long kept hidden
Coercing my vulnerabilities into the light
I floundered to find my bearings
As I listened to your words
Wondered if I even wanted to close the gash
Or if I should just leave it open
Never allow it to scar over
It opened me to so much
A slash, a gash
Compassion learned
So thank you so much for speaking those words
As painful as they were as they penetrated my being

Divided

My heart divided in two
Half frozen solid
Half blazing flames
Competing for dominance
Passion melts fear
Terror freezes desire
The frozen side a fortress
Tempering the burning need within
I fight the incompatibility of me
My blazing, freezing heart
Reaches for you
Freezes you out
Burns you up
A flame of passion
Reaches into the ice
To be frozen in place by vulnerability
Dying to live with my whole heart
Instead of toggling
My burning passion
My freezing vulnerability
Fearing my thawed vulnerability
Will burn the whole thing to cinders
Fearing my freezing passion
Will ignite every vulnerability
I hold tight to both halves of my divided heart
Incompatible though they may appear
Warring to conquer
My vulnerability, my passion
My fire, my ice

Love Reaches for Trust

Love reached for trust's hand
Trust's hand shook with hesitation
Trust knew if it took love's hand
A commitment would be made
Vulnerability would be exposed
Not taking love's hand promised no gain
Trust weighed the risk
Reached slowly toward love's proffered hand
Scared love would jerk it back at the last minute
But, love, oh, love held steady
Love waited for trust
Once love and trust held hands
Divinity glowed from their union

Reflection in Tears

I am stronger than this
Damn it
I know I am
I will not allow this
I whispered these words
To the empty room
Even as
My shoulders pulled in
My breath became shallow
My heart raced then failed me
My skin became sensitive
My thoughts lost cohesiveness
My emotions melted
I heard her words and hers and hers
My story through the voice of so many others
Remnants that match
Yet each different in its own way
Reactions I know all too well
Ones I've contained as best I could
Ones I've denied even to myself
Ones I've struggled to understand
And that look in all those eyes
The tears flowing
Reflecting me back to me
In the walls I recognize
Around hearts, souls, bodies
We are survivors
Beneath an armor of pain and betrayal
Trapping us within ourselves
Containing us within our pain
Denying us a break from the

Reflection so prevalent in the
Tears we share

Trigger City

Trigger City
Somehow, someway
No matter how high I build the walls
No matter how deep I dig the moat
No matter how many locks I put on the doors
I find myself dropped smack dab
In Trigger City
Bombarded by reminder upon reminder
Words spoken
A smell evokes
A touch to that sensitive spot
A feeling tapped into
Leaving me crying in the middle of
Trigger City
Wishing you'd never known me
Or
I'd never known you
Triggers shot from automatic weapons
Hitting me right in the heart
Shrapnel cutting through my skin
Inundated by triggers
Until I'm curled up in a ball
Until I'm holding my breath
Until I'm sobbing uncontrollably
Eventually I crawl out of
Trigger City
Close the door, add another lock
Build another fortress
Dig a deeper moat
Promise myself there's no way
I'm returning to

Trigger City
Knowing even as I make the promise
There's nothing I can do
To avoid my visits to
Trigger City
No matter how hard I try
Trigger City lives deep inside me
Uninhabitable in the best of times
Indestructible in the worst of times
The things beyond my control
That unlock the door
That scale the fortress walls
That swim the moat
All in a matter of seconds
Beyond my control
I just have to accept
I have no power over
Trigger City

Triggers

Triggers
An image
A sound
A smell
A touch
A taste
That's all it takes
The moment floods back
Fear overwhelms me
My body refuses movement

Triggers
A word
A story
A joke
A phrase
A comment
A breath
That's all it takes
The pain floods back
Powerlessness overwhelms me
My body shakes uncontrollably

Triggers
Releasing bullets
Ripping my life apart
Dreams that suffocate
Memories that imprison me
Fears that dissolve me
My body flinches at the slightest touch

Triggers
Just when I think
I'm strong enough
To not be affected
The world reminds me
Complacency can't happen
My shield goes back up
My survival depends on it
My ability to thrive depends on it
My body never forgets
Triggers

Hunted

Your promise to always find me
Haunted me, haunts me still
I hid behind miles
Ran to the ends of ledges
Jumped off cliffs
Left ashes in place of bridges
Severed lifelines long cherished
Escaped memories created
Flew through clouds of soft landings
Drowned in promises for the future
Suffocated in pillows of possibility
Never believing I was safe
On I ran
Across the continent
Across the seas
Across the skies
Through forests
Through deserts
Through cities
Disappeared into myself
Denied my own existence
Delegated my life to others
All because you planted a seed
I couldn't escape
A seed of being
Hunted

Dark Spot

There's a dark spot
In my soul
It only comes out when
I remember
So I do everything I can
To forget
There's a dark spot
In my heart
It only reveals itself
When you sneak into my emotions
So I do everything I can
To never feel your presence
There's a dark spot
In my mind
It only appears
When you capture my thoughts
So I do everything I can
To never think of you
There's a dark spot
In my life
It only appears when
I stop moving
So I do everything I can
To never cease movement
There's a dark spot…
You created it…
You own it…
You said I'd never forget you…
You were right
I always remember you
As the dark spot

Tainting my love
Darkening my soul
Invading my thoughts
Capturing my life
No matter how much light I capture
You always find a way back in
Through those crevices of vulnerability
Where you hide when I'm strong
Awaiting a weak moment
To reveal yourself
My light shines too bright
For your dark spot to rule me
So I accept you for what you are
Nothing more than
A dark spot
In an otherwise bright being

The Look

One look in your eyes
You cannot hide
The frozen tundra
Living inside
Freezing you to yourself
Scars adorn your skin
Welts decorate your soul
Burns lace your heart
Little pricks of you oozing out of your pores
The quakes brought on by a touch, however gentle
Breathing crushes your chest
The body remembers every
Blow inflicted
No matter how hard the mind
Tries to forget
Reliving the moment
In flashbacks of great terror
Or small reactions of panic
Either way it's always there
You never escape
What you experience
You only learn to manage it
To manage yourself
And try to find a moment of growth within
In order to not feel consumed by the injustice
Of pain inflicted
I recognize the look
It's all too familiar

Isolation

You took me away
Just as I requested
I wanted to hide
I wanted to find something new
I wanted a place where no one knew me before…
You accommodated my wish
You took me away
Little did I know
Isolation would soon follow
Friends abandoned
Family estranged
As I hid from my fears
As I retreated from life
Under the guise of building
A new life
A new beginning
A new me
The isolation I embraced
As my fortress
As my protection
As my chance
Soon transformed into
My prison
My solitary confinement
My loss of me
One day I woke up
Smothered
Strangled
Dead inside
I'd come to hate
My isolation

Cost

I gave you everything I could
Yet it was never enough
I always knew I held back
I couldn't help it
I wanted to give you all of me
But my mind refused to give
What my heart wanted to offer
So I watched as I held my vulnerability
In that safe place behind my open façade
Unable to release it
I prayed you'd never search behind my smile
I never wanted you to see how easily you could hurt me
So I gave you something bright and shiny
To glare above the darkness lurking within
Dressed up in faux glitter
As I prayed to a god I no longer believed in
That you'd see beyond my surface
To the depths hiding within
I struggled to reveal my truth to you
As I watched you drift away
On a sea of regrets we never fulfilled
Taking the possibility of us with you
I stopped fighting the current
Drifted under the surface into the depths of me
Only to discover
My truth was stronger than I ever realized
As I embraced my vulnerability
Bringing the glow of honesty to my surface
Releasing me to the world
And all it cost me
Was

You...

Silence

Silence layers between us
As life progresses
We talk about everything
Everything except what matters
We nurture silence because
It keeps us from vulnerability
We have built walls
That allow us to stay together
Without truly connecting
We sit without words
Deceiving ourselves silence is intimacy
A deception we need to not disintegrate
Silence keeps reality from interfering
With life's daily movements
Giving us reasons to ignore our pain
Ignoring yesterday's truth
In favor of today's fiction
As life pushes us toward tomorrow
We try to forget yesterday
Only to find the silence we cultivated
Dying in the soil we devotedly toiled
Deception and truth cannot grow together
Even when, especially when
Fertilized by silence

Begging

Go ahead
Slam that door between us
That's your prerogative
Just remember
I'm done begging
Opening it again will be up to you
Just be prepared if you slam it often enough
I'll lock it and refuse you entry
You have to know that every time
You strike out at me
You shut me out
You ignore me
I place another lock on the door
You'll find it becomes
More and more difficult to open
With every slam
I know my worth
I refuse to deny my worth
I embrace my worth
When you treat me less than I deserve
I have no problem leaving that door shut
So be careful
When you decide to take your frustration out on me
Begging is no longer part of my repertoire
Love me or leave me
I'll survive either way
Hell, I'll thrive either way
But I will never again beg you to love me

Stubborn

I am stubborn
Often to my own detriment
I refuse to see reality
Even when it slaps me in the face
My stubbornness has cost me plenty
Left me flailing in a field of loss
Clinging to blooms of memory
Wishing for roots that result in new plants
Seeds dropping from memory
To create new possibilities
Wrapped in old regrets
And, yet, when I've decided
I don't back down
I don't give up
I don't give in
I'll find a way to protect what's left of me
Rather than risk all that could be
I'll stay and fight even when I'm exhausted
Rather than admit I can't win
If only I wasn't so incredibly stubborn
I've been told
Changing a mule's mind is easier than changing mine
And yet
Where has all my stubborn protectiveness gotten me
Protected and going through the motions
Exhausted and trudging on in the pointless
Dreaming every night of relenting to you
Wishing I had the courage to give up my pride
Longing for you to reach out and coax open
The stubborn fortress I've build to protect me
The fortress I fight to protect to the point of collapse

The fortress I fight to keep in place to protect me
From my heart's desires

Dissolve

Thank you
For not letting me disappear
For holding me in place
When I feel myself dissolving
For thinking I'm awesome
When I'm sure I'm awful
For reaching out
When I pull away
For wanting me to be happy
When my life is imploding
For wanting me to smile
When all I want is to cry
For making me laugh
When life isn't fun
For reminding me
Of my inner strength
For not allowing me to be erased
By those who would rather I not be me
For encouraging me to
Stand up for myself
For pushing me to
Be my best self
Nothing more, nothing less
For reminding me
I don't have to be perfect
I don't' have to fit anyone's image
I don't have to give up me
To be loved
I don't have to dissolve
To find a place in life
I only have to be me

And
Anyone who tries to
Dissolve me
Doesn't deserve me

Need

I may want you
I may love you
But I'll never need you
I'm sorry
In all honesty
Wanting you doesn't scare me
Loving you unnerves me a bit
But
Needing you terrifies me
I can want you and leave you
I can love you and set you free
If I need you, you might break my heart
Don't ask me for more than I can give
And, maybe just maybe
I'll figure out a way to lower my defenses
And let you come in for a visit
A long visit if you can
Accept me as I am
And let me find my way
Without trying to fix me
And, understand when I say
I want you to
Want me
Love me
Need me
Even though I can't need you back
At least not right now…

Reach

Reach inside my soul
Pull out my secrets
Reach inside my heart
Pull out my desires
Reach inside my mind
Pull out my intelligence
Reach inside my core
Pull out my creativity
Reach inside my body
Pull out my life
Reach inside
Pull out... me
If you think you can handle what you find

Devours

Your energy devours mine
Leaves me starving
Takes all I have to give
Leaves me desperate
Takes the breath from my lungs
Leaves me gasping
Takes the love from my heart
Leaves me empty
Takes the joy from my soul
Leaves me drained
Takes the smile from my lips
Leaves me searching
Takes the laughter from my mouth
Leaves me crying
Takes the passion from my words
Leaves me blocked
Your energy devours mine
Leaves me dead

Decision

I've made a decision
You're not going to like it
My brain knows I'm right
The risk must be taken
My heart questions me
Are you sure?
My soul understands my need
I must take care of me
I struggle to tell you
The words won't come
I can't bear to hurt you
When the words finally take form
I know what'll happen
Or at least I think I know
You may surprise me with your response
I hope against hope you will
But the decision had to made
And you kept hinting then hesitating
So I made a decision
That puts me
In control of my life
And leaves you
To find your place in it

Chasing

I will catch you
No matter what
That's what I promised
I chased you
As long as I could
But your demons took you
So far away
My words failed to reach you
My touch only frightened you
My love only coddled your delusions
My concern excused your behavior
I caught you for years
I held your hand
I listened to your heartache
I helped you every way I knew how
Then one day exhaustion claimed me
I had my own life to live
I had my own problems to fix
I had to let you go
You ran toward a place
I couldn't exist
And I knew it
I had no choice but to let you go
Because chasing you
Had started to
Destroy me

Numb

I went numb
Numb was easier
Easier than life
Life brought only pain
Pain never stopped
Stopped to let me breathe
Breathe in a full clear breath of fresh air
Air to energize my thoughts
Thoughts to keep me engaged
Engaged in the neverending whirlwind
Whirlwind in my heart
Heart filled with memories
Memories of how I got to the place
Place where numbness felt better
Better than living

Inky Night

The inky night
Spreads across my life
Casting all in shadow
Hiding deceptions from the light
Erasing delusions of trust
Upending security
Untethering the vulnerability
Relieving my need
Acknowledging my desire
Taking me hostage
Unearthing that best left buried
Yet my heart continues to love

Prison of Love

Did you always consider
My love a prison?
Something designed to
Entrap you
Kidnap you
Confine you
Was there ever a moment
You appreciated all I offered?
When I lavished you
With attention
When I gave up
My goals
When I sacrificed
My inner self
When I weakened
My inner strength
When I quashed
My self-esteem
When I gave you
Everything I was
When I twisted myself
Into the woman you said you wanted
When I opened
My heart to you
When I exposed
My soul to you
When I shared
My innermost fears with you
When I revealed
My deepest, darkest secrets to you
When I turned my heart

Over to your hands
When I willingly handed you
My soul
When I gave you control
Of my needs
When I bared my being
To your whims
I suppose that's a prison
If you say so
Now you tell me
My desire to
Be cherished
My need to
Feel valued
My craving to
Be respected
My longing
To be adored
My yearning
To be your only love
Felt like prison to you
And yet I don't think
I'm so different
Than any other human being
So maybe it wasn't my love
That imprisoned you
Did you ever consider that?

Giving Up

If you really knew me
You'd know I don't give up
Even when hurled words
Shatter my heart like a window
Bruising the love within on impact
Releasing my vulnerabilities
To spill like salty rain from clouds above
Soaking the floor of my soul
As I search for a reason to hate
All I find is the love that drives me
To dry the floor
To heal the bruise
To repair the window
Because to give in to hate
Destroys my foundation
So I'd rather fix what can be fixed a million times
Than to give up on love
I'd rather be in constant need of repair
Than to never risk the possibilities love offers

Playful Side

You never liked
The playful side of me
When she appeared
You always quashed her
With seriousness
With misunderstanding
You mocked her
Until I retreated
Until I quashed her for you
Until I became serious
Until I quit trying
I miss
The playful side of me
The side that would
Tease you
Tempt you
Play word games with you
Crack funny at your seriousness
Coax a smile from your set lips
You never accepted
The playful side of me
With her open sensuality
Dirty jokes
Flirtatious nature
"Who gives a damn?" attitude
"Let's just do it." approach
You looked at her
With open disdain
Disapproval in your eyes
Reprimand in your voice
Expectations in your words

Demands in your actions
You held your love hostage
Awaiting my capitulation
To kill
The playful side of me
After her demise
You asked
Why I was no longer fun…

Favorite Failure

I am your
Failure
My attempts
Failed your
Expectations
My efforts to be
What you desired
Never quite enough
Yet you see my choice
To morph in order to please
As a failure instead of a sacrifice
I gave up my sense of me
In order to please you
And yet in the end
I remain
Your failure
Perhaps your
Favorite failure
But your failure nonetheless

The Forest of Me

As you explore
The dark forest
That is me
Perhaps you will see
The twisting, turning path
That is my mind
Perhaps you will feel
The dense fog
That is my soul
Perhaps you will touch
The tall, reaching trees
That are my veins
Perhaps you will find
The hidden light
That is my heart
Perhaps you will uncover
The strength, the beauty, the intelligence
That lives within my skin
Perhaps you will feel me
Consume you whole
As you become lost in
The dark forest
That is forever me

Flowing

Flowing from my heart
Emanating from my soul
Reaching out to you
Touching all between us
Your words reveal you to me
Your support lifts me up
Your silence frightens me
My silence hides me
My support is yours for the taking
My words offer me to you
Will you accept?
Do you see?
Do you hear?
Do you know?
Will I ever be brave enough
To reveal the full truth
Hidden in the recesses of my heart
I search for the courage in my solitude
And run from it when I find it
I hide from the truth of what I feel
Every time it refuses to be denied
I long for you to reach for me
I just hope you won't wait too long
Only to discover I've disappeared
Because
When you look at me
I feel your affection
Flow from your heart
Yet I fear I deceive myself
Because I so want
Love for me to

Flow from your heart
And join the love for you that
Flows from my heart
Imagine if
The love
Flowing from your heart
And
The love
Flowing from my heart
Joined
Our love would overwhelm
The world
With goodness
With light
With positivity
So I open my heart
Pray you can feel
The love
Flow from my heart
Reaching out
For the love
Flowing from your heart
Because together
You and I allowing
Our love to
Flow from our hearts
Would ripple through
Time and space
Creating a wave filled with
Promise

The Muse

I fear
Without the pain
I have nothing to say

I fear
Without the anguish
I'll lose the words

I fear
Without derision
The words will betray me

I fear
Without anger
My words will bore

I fear
Without sadness
There's nothing to share

I fear
Without turmoil
My work will suffer

I fear
Without angst
Inspiration will disappear

I fear
Without drama
I won't matter

Left of Me

If I offered you
What's left of me
Would that be enough
Or would you demand more
Would you try to reassemble
The building blocks of me
One damaged block at a time
Or would you see the perfection
In the scattered bits of me
Floating unfettered
Building upon themselves
Creating a new version
Complete with missing pieces
Where those vulnerable bits disintegrated
Leaving me with an incomplete
Version of me to give
Or perhaps you'll not see
The missing bits
And find what I have left to offer
Quite enough

Pitcher

This outline of me
Looks up at a pitcher
Filled with life
Ready to fill
My heart with love
Read to expand
My soul with joy
Ready to inspire
My brain with thoughts
Ready to strengthen
My body with experience
Ready to infuse
My being with generosity
As life pours from the pitcher
Into the outline of me
Color radiates from me
Takes me from
One dimensional to three dimensional
Morphing me from outline
To human being

Survival

Push me to the edge
Once again
See how strong I really am
I'll cling to
Every rock
Every branch
Every leaf
Every speck of dust
The thin air, if need be
I'll close my eyes
Sprout wings, if need be
Reach toward the sky
Plant my feet for a landing
Ready myself for impact
What I won't do, can't do
Is crumble like mud turned to dust
I just can't do that
My need to survive reigns too strong
I'll call on every ounce of strength I possess
To stand tall in the face of whatever
You throw at me
I'll catch it with my bare hands
No matter how much it hurts
Store it away in the recesses of my heart
Where it'll be safe from harm
Hide it away in the depths of my mind
Where it'll be safe from discovery
But through it all
Teetering on the edge of the cliff
I'll stand shoulders squared
Until I fall
And then I'll search for a path

To land safely
Stronger for the
Survival

Drops of Love

Drops of love
Pounding against my body
Soaking my skin
Muddying my conviction to release you
Filling the voids in my heart
Left behind with the loss of connection
Radiating peace into the atmosphere
Reminding me that love liberates
Taking me high enough to touch the clouds
Releasing my inhibitions
Relieving my fears
Soothing my vulnerabilities
Showing me we can be so much more
I stand with my arms wide open, face to the sky
Welcoming the sensation
As love pours into my being
Each drop of love
Opening my heart to possibility
Gently showing me pain heals
Relieving my need to fight
Creating peace
And I wonder
Do you stand with arms wide open, face to the sky
Welcoming the sensation
As you're pounded by
Drops of love

All of Me

If I gave you
All of me
Would you recognize
The treasure
You received
Or would you think
Me a useless adornment
If I offered you
All of me
Would you accept
The specialness
Before you
Or would you think
Me ordinary
If I presented
All of me
Would you realize
Your good fortune
Or would you think
Me worthless
If I revealed
All of me
Would you embrace
The perfection in my imperfection
Or would you think
My flaws fatal
If I risked
All of me
Would you cherish
My generous heart and spirit
Or would you think

Me too needy
If I opened
All of me
Would you love me
Just as I am
Or would you
Leave

Paled

My eyes peek out from behind
Black lace seeing all I fear
I avoid looking in your eyes
Knowing the void I'll see there
The pain we inflicted
Paled our essences
Masked our individual selves
Made us mere puppets of
The people we once were
Without knowing it
We lost what we most loved
Even while standing together
We faced the future
Hiding from each other
Hiding from ourselves
Hiding from the world
Trying so desperately
To embrace the beauty
Of the bright red rose that was once love
Shining against our paleness
Shining against our blackness
My eyes searching for the strength I lost
Yours hollow with the drain of sacrifice
Love now feels more like a thorn than a bright red rose
The path before us is dull and gray like a rainy day
We cling to one another
Hoping it isn't too late to
Reclaim all we've lost in our quest
To hold on to the dream
Of the life we never really lived

Searching the World

Upon a wave of *wunsch*
I rode in search of *amour*
Instead I found myself awash
In a sea of *odio*
I searched for respite
Among the natives
Of country after country
Returning home unable to understand
How I could continue to *contestare*
Everything the world offered me even
As I failed to accept the truth
See in the end, until I could accept me
It mattered not what the world offered
The day I stepped into myself
Said to the world
Accept me as I am
Amour me as I am
Odio me if you must
Contestare me if you must
For I can only be me
Wunsch lifted me higher
And the world said
Shukran
For giving me
The only gift you could ever offer…
You
Shukran, World

This Heart of Mine

This heart of mine
Shattered
Splintered
Broken
Smashed
Crushed
Shredded
A million times over
This heart of mine
Rebuilt every single time
By the resolve to stand strong
By the desire to be cherished
By the hope of love
This heart of mine
May be battered and bruised
May be covered with scars
May have lost the beauty of newness
But it remains resilient
This heart of mine
I offer willingly
I give freely
I risk openly
Because someday
You will see beyond
The scars of yesterday
To the delicacy within
To the truth of me
To the love hiding inside
I have faith that when
I hand you
This heart of mine

You'll hold it gently
You'll treat its wounds
You'll cherish its scars
You'll see its beauty
You'll respect its memories
So I hold
This heart of mine
With shaking hands
Waiting to present it to you
Wondering if my trust
Will be betrayed
But knowing it'll break
Just as much, maybe even more
If I never risk it

You Scare Me

You scare me
Your disarming smile
The love in your eyes
The desire in your fingertips
The intimacy you request
You want to know me
All of me
Nothing scares me more
Than showing you my vulnerability
When you really know me
You know how to hurt me
When you really know me
You know how to destroy me
When you really know me
You know how to possess me
When you really know me
You know my strength and my weakness
You just might not like what you find
And while I usually don't care if other people like me
You're different
I want you to love me
I want you to need me
I want you to want me
I want you to cherish me
So I have to admit
When you reach out
And try to know me
You scare me

Vulnerable

Uncover me now
Expose my experience
Leave me wide open

Walking into Me

Walking into me
Looking to be free
Bumped and bruised
Ego red and inflamed
Not thinking too highly of me
Seeing how I can be
When life takes a turn
That leaves a burn
Upon my heart
Forcing a new start
Lost in my scars
Running from stars
Fresh cuts bleed
Upon which I feed
Stumbling into you
With all my icky goo
Overflowing with hope
You'll throw me a saving rope
Knowing even as I suffocate
Only I can save my fate
Hold on tight
As I run into the dark night
Someday I'll be ready
Standing steady
Can you wait for me
To be what you already see?

Pieces

The pieces fit
Move them
Cajole them
Manipulate them
They land in front of me
The maze of my life
Pieces that move faster than light
Morphing as fast as they appear
Leaving me changed
Staring at pieces that make no sense
Leave gaps I cannot fill
Allowing a view into my soul
Where all my vulnerabilities thrive
Fed by the morphing pieces
Flying, flowing, flexing
Into my life
Demanding my attention
As I move from one moment to the next
Feeling my need to fill the voids
To address the emptiness in me
When I excise the pieces that don't fit
I make room for the pieces that do
Creating a structure on which I stand
Filled with strength
Filled with purpose
As I search for the pieces that complete me

Lens

Hold my breath
Wait
Hold my pose
Wait
Listen for the click
A moment captured
Through your lens
Is it real?
Posed though it may be
It's still a moment shared
You show me the image you captured
Is that how you see me?
Is that how I look?
Is that reality?
Is that fantasy?
I move into position
Wait
Hold my breath
Wait
For you to capture me
In your lens
Creating an image
In my likeness
That reflects
Your vision
As I scream
Wait!
That's not me…
Or maybe it's more me than I know

Hug Me Tightly

Hugs heal our hearts
Unveiling the strength within
Granting us power to change

Mend my discombobulated
Escaping energy

Taking me to new heights
Insisting I embrace the love
Gilded by the armor I built
High enough to guard my heart
Tough enough to keep vulnerability out
Lifting me to release the shackles
You unlocked with your hug

…Hug me tightly

Copper

Bright copper
Tarnished around the edges
Weathered and exposed
Revealing a sense of history
Bringing a beautiful new patina to life
The brightness dulls
Revealing a new depth
Character exposed
Copper shines bright
Reflecting light and warmth
Shades of green patina
Slowly conquering the shine
Leaving only remnants
Of what once was
Revealing beauty
Rarely remains the same

Sparkles Hiding

Black velvet
Sparkles hiding underneath
Waiting for your discovery
You lift my leg
Your hand on my calf
Your touch gentle
My calf flexed
My heel spikes the air
A weapon
An enticement
The crystals underneath draw your eye
As the light reflects their depths
You turn
Your eyes stare into mine
The sparkle there
In yours and mine
Outshines those crystals
You see
My soul
Also black velvet
Sparkles hiding underneath
Awaiting your discovery

Fear Traps Us

Fear traps us
Traps us in place
Places us in prison
Imprisons our minds
Minds our emotions
Emotes around us a moat
A moat to keep out love
Love lost in the depths
Depths of the intense fear
Fear keeps us trapped
Trapped in fear's embrace

Blender

You dropped my heart in a blender
Pureed it into a thick smoothie
Poured it into a cracked, crystal glass
Left it on the counter, forgotten
I cried bloody tears
As I struggled to reassemble
My blended heart
Into a solid mass again
No matter how I manipulated it
I could never get back its original form
So my heart remains
Messy, scarred, mushy
But blended though it may be
All the tiny pulverized pieces remain
Even it if can't beat quite in rhythm
Even if the blood doesn't quite flow through it
Even if it barely resembles itself
The beats search for the rhythm
The blood trickles through
It remembers its former self
Someday I'm sure I'll figure out
How to rescue my heart before
Someone decides to
Drop it in a blender
Pulverize it
Pour it in a cracked glass
Leave it on the counter, forgotten
Until then all I can do
Is figure out how to heal
The smoothie you created
When you dropped my heart in a blender

Rip Me to Shreds

Rip me to shreds
Sort out the pieces
Tape me back together
Tatters and tears
Frazzled and frayed
Leaving me almost
As I was

Rip me to shreds
Sort out the pieces
Glue me back together
Tatters and tears
Frazzled and frayed
Leaving me almost
As I was

Rip me to shreds
Sort out the pieces
Sew me back together
Tatters and tears
Frazzled and frayed
Leaving me almost
As I was

Rip me to shreds
You can try
I'm tough to shred
Tatters and tears
Frazzled and frayed
Leaving me almost
As I was

Back to You

It may appear I've turned my back to you
But I'm really showing you I trust you
This is when I feel most vulnerable
When I cannot see your actions
When I can only feel your touch
When I can only hear your breath
When I can only smell your closeness
When you can leave without my knowledge
When you can inflict pain I can't predict
When your movement is yours alone
When you choose how to treat me
When you discover the unspoken message
My heart pounds in anticipation
I can't help but peek over my shoulder to see
What comes next now that
I've given you my complete trust

Someone Knows

Your words accost
Your eyes sear
Your voice pierces
The anger within
Seeps out
Hidden beneath
Smiles that bewitch
Eyes that shine
Meaningless platitudes
Years of hiding
Even from yourself
Public faces
Private thoughts
Transformed
Searching

Needing to know
Who you are
Reaching out
Hiding away
Thinking no one knows
Your pain
Your frustration
Your anger
Your sadness
Your nothingness
Someone knows
Someone cares

The Real You

Stand up
Speak
Tell me what you believe
Not what you think I want to hear
What you really believe
Your truth may not be my truth
But that makes it no less important
Show me the real you
Not who you think I want to see
Your real self
Give me your thoughts
Good and bad
I want it all
Don't hold back
I want to know you
Whoever you are
I want to see all of you
Not just what you think will earn my approval
To love you
I need to know you
All of you
No matter how we disagree
If you're real
I'll accept you
Be yourself
And so will I
We may not be perfect
But we'll be real
We may not even like each other
But at least that will be truth
Stand up

Don't hide behind convention and manners
Be true
Be real
Be honest
Be yourself above all else

Needy

You think because I smile
I am happy
You think because I laugh
I am amused
You think because I always give you my shoulder
I have no problems
You think because I always listen
I have no sorrows hidden in my heart
You think because I don't ask for help
I can handle it on my own
You think because I don't cry in front of you
I don't hurt
You think because I nod and keep silent
I have nothing to say
You think because I don't ask for you to hold me
I don't need you
You think because I don't complain
I have a perfect life
You see what you want to see
And I let you
So I don't have to let you
See me as vulnerable
See me as weak
See me as needy

Not That You Asked

Not that you asked
But in case you were wondering
Yes, I needed a friend
More to the point, I needed you
A simple "How are you?"
Would've meant the world
A simple "I'm thinking about you"
Would've brightened my day
A simple "I'm here if you need me"
Would've changed so very much

Not that you asked
But in case you were wondering
That day I listened while you complained
I needed to be heard, too
I cried all day
My heart was breaking
From words that ripped my life apart
Words you knew nothing about
And you added to my pain
Without once asking
"How are things with you?"

Not that you asked
But in case you were wondering
No, my life isn't perfect
There are days when I feel like giving up
Just like you
I feel all my efforts are wasted
Of course, you'd know that
If you ever asked

"How are your projects coming along?

Not that you asked
But in case you were wondering
Yes, I needed a friend
More to the point, I needed you
When everything was falling apart
When life cracked my foundation
When I faltered and didn't know where to turn
But again you'd know that
If you'd once bothered to ask
"Do you need to talk?"

Not that you asked
But in case you were wondering
I'm doing much better now
And I did it without your help
When I felt most alone
A stranger reminded me
I didn't have to face my pain alone
I would've preferred you ask
"What can I do?"

Not that you asked
But in case you were wondering
Yes, I needed a friend
More to the point I needed you
But now
I don't
So don't bother to ask
"Want to spend some time together?"

Embracing My Desire

I should
I shouldn't
Who cares if I do
Who cares if I don't
Will it matter if I do
Will it matter if I don't
This dilemma runs on a loop in my thoughts
Whenever I consider my desires
My deep down desires
The ones I hold in my secret room
The ones sometimes even I fear
The ones that expose too much of me
What's the worst thing that happens
If I unleash my desires on the world
I suppose someone, even me, might get hurt
Or perhaps those desires will liberate someone, even me
Yet I always question my desires
Tamp them down
Fight them
Ignore them
Finally I've come to realize
My endless dilemma loop occurs because
I fear the power inherent in my desires
And, really, truly, what is there to fear?

Frozen Ashes

Better to burn up in flames of ice
Or freeze in frozen fire
Than to stay locked in this fortress
Where ice never melts
Where fire never burns
Where ice burns
Where fire freezes
Numbness freezes the world
Numbness burns possibility
Life moves forward
Leaving me frozen in a fire
That seeks to devour me whole
All I can do is watch
Knowing the decision I made
Matters more than I knew
Regret changes nothing
So I sink into the frozen fire
We created and wait
For the ashes of me to freeze

Depths of Me

You reached into
The depths of me
Pulled my heart out of the muck
Washed away debris from its scars
Caressed my needs
With gentle teases
Until I moaned
And begged you
To go deeper
Massaged my insecurities
With firm pressure
Moving deeper
With each touch
Held my vulnerability
With a loving grip
Delving deeper
With each squeeze
You showed me
Deep didn't have to
Sever
Destroy
Scar
Deep can
Heal
Create
Satiate

Inside This Place

Inside this place
Where I stand
Looking out
Searching
Frozen in place
Looking inward
Reaching out
Crying for release
Wishing for liberty
Begging for life
Longing for laughter
Needing to be whole
Emoting my desire
Standing still
Looking out
From
Inside this place

Just Beneath My Murky Top

Just beneath my pain
Bubbles of laughter
Churn and burn
Expand and blister
Shimmer and burst
Just beneath my laughter
Bubbles of pain
Burst and bleed
Ripple and burn
Scab and scar
Just beneath my pain
My smile hides
Ready to burst forth
Ready to shine
Ready to welcome you
Just beneath my smile
My pain flutters
Ready to dissipate
Ready to forgive
Ready to forget
Just beneath my façade
Lies the heart of me
All yours
If you're brave enough
To reach
Just beneath my murky top
To find
The pure heart concealed

Cactus Cannot Become a Vine

I present
Only who I am
It's all I've got
When you ask me to forget
What makes me me
You ask too much
You forget
You once proclaimed love for me
You once worshipped me
When I gave in to your demands
I forgot
Love withers and dies
When forced into too small a pot
The roots twist round and round
Strangling the core
Love withers and dies
When fed little drops of poisonous words
Day after day wrapped in the best intentions
Dripping with sweetness but still damaging
Love withers and dies
When the beloved tries to change
The core of its being
A cactus can never become a vine
It is impossible to survive
When treated as someone one isn't
The cactus watered as a vine will rot
The vine planted in cactus soil will never thrive
The cactus fertilized as a vine will not grow
The vine denied water as if a cactus will dry up
A cactus cannot be treated as a vine
It will die

So when you try to change me
You risk killing
The very thing you claim to love
But if what you want is a cactus
Why did you bring home a vine?

Barbed Wire Fortress

You opened your soul to me
Without seeing the barbed wire
Surrounding mine
You came closer
Reaching out
Ignoring the barbed wire
Imprisoning my soul
I tried to warn you
But I wanted you near me
So much
The words wouldn't form
I watched as you
Wrapped your hand
Around the barbed wire
The barbs drew your blood
You didn't even flinch
You gently
Pulled the barbed wire from my soul
I felt the barbs rip the
Scarred surface off my soul
My blood dripping next to yours
My vulnerabilities exposed
I gasped as I searched your face
Compassion and determination
Flooded your expression
Perhaps love was what you offered
Dare I hope?
I reached for the bloody barbed wire
Fear threatened freedom
The barbed wire was familiar
It kept me in

It kept everyone else out
It kept you out
How could I live without it?
It had become a part of me
But you
You tossed it into the air
Where it disintegrated into dust
I stared unbelieving
Felt the healing power
Of the open wounds on my soul
I looked into your eyes and
Readied my heart
To be freed from
Its barbed wire fortress

Loved From a Distance

Tonight I looked at my life
As is
Without filter
Or so I thought
Everyone who loves me is far away
Really loves me
Not likes me
Not needs me
Not wants something from me
But who loves me unconditionally
No one stays near
Not even…
No one comes to me
Everyone asks me to visit
Everyone asks me to come
People laugh with me
Share stories with me
Misery and laughter rolled up together
No one suggests I stay
People reach out
Pull away
Begin strong
Overwhelm me with what they see in me
Get to know me
Leave
Perhaps the message is
Perhaps what I don't want to know is
Perhaps what I can't accept is
Perhaps what I fear is
I can only be truly
Loved from a distance

The Fortress Behind My Smile

My smile
Welcomes you
Invites you to come closer
Teases you with knowing me
Offers you a sense of comfort
Radiates brighter than the sun
Or so someone special once said
Though I never quite believed that one
But when you step a little closer
You see the smile conceals a well built fortress
There behind my smile my armor remains intact
When you attempt to penetrate the fortress
An army of defensive tactics meets you
Silence fends you off
Cutting words cast shadows across the brilliance
Swords of doubt slice through your charm
Guns shoot holes through your loving gestures
I've learned to protect the core of me
From you and all others who would invade
The fortress behind my smile
In search of my love
In search of my heart
In search of my truth
Your invasion has the potential
To shatter my defenses
To leave me open to vulnerability
To risk my strength
So I hide behind my fortress
As my smile tricks you into believing
You know me
You love me

You want me
You need me
Until the moment you're driven to penetrate
The fortress behind my sweet, seductive smile

In the Dark

My love for you resides
In the dark
Where it belongs
It hides in the shadows
Awaiting a sliver of light
Denied existence by the inky night
Unblemished by the light of stars
Unbroken by the beams of the moon
Unseen by prying eyes
When I dream
Your love shines so bright
In the dark recesses of my heart
Where no one dares tread – not even me
In the dark
When I close my eyes
Against the darkness where I live
Your love denies my darkness
Takes me on a journey
To the light inside me
Until I close the door once again
So darkness reigns across my being
Turning my every smile into subterfuge
Light hiding the darkness within

In Case Of

In case of romance
Call my brain
Remind my heart
Romance shades the truth
From reality
Allowing me to blind myself
With fantasy
Immersing myself in the sweet nectar
That tricks me into believing
Lust is love

In case of betrayal
Call my heart
Remind my brain
Vulnerability rewards risks
With reality
Allowing me to find truth
In fantasy
Dipping me in bitter ale
That raises my fortresses
Betrayal creates hate

In case of hate
Call my brain
Remind my heart
Hate destroys truth
With lies
Allowing me to exact judgment
On reality
Trapping me in bitter ale
That drowns my compassion

Hate destroys love

In case of love
Call my heart
Remind my brain
Love illuminates truth
From fantasy
Allowing me to envision
A reality
Releasing me from the sweet nectar
Allowing me to understand
Love transcends life itself

Find Me Waiting

Find me there
Where life intersects death
On the path to everywhere and nowhere
Waiting for you to join me
Waiting for you to see me
Waiting for you to love me
Find me there
Where strength meets weakness
On the path to awareness and denial
Waiting for you to join me
Waiting for you to see me
Waiting for you to love me
Find me there
Where love meets hate
On the path to happiness and sadness
Waiting for you to join me
Waiting for you to see me
Waiting for you to love me
Find me there
Where tomorrow meets yesterday
On the path to always and forever
Waiting for you to join me
Waiting for you to see me
Waiting for you to love me
Find me there
On the path…
Waiting…

Would You

What if
I let my heart truly dictate
I let go of my fear
I found the courage
I didn't parse the words
I didn't hide from my truth
I opened myself to you
I allowed you to see
I tore down the fortress
I lost all protective pretense
I embraced my hidden strength
I revealed my scariest vulnerability
I took the risk
I spoke those words
Would you do the same?

Proactive Waiting

I let go
I released
The grip I held
On
What yesterday meant
What today holds
What tomorrow will bring
I released my desires
To that beyond my control
I accepted my role in my own life
Active participant
Not bystander
Not all powerful
I must do my part
And trust the rest will come my way
The place I belong
The people I need
The role I must play
The change in front of me
The truth of who I am
When I released my power
The power around me
Overwhelmed my fear of tomorrow
Offered me a chance to live in this moment
Filled me with the faith I shall have my heart's desires
If only I trust life to provide for me
If only I relax enough to see the opportunity
If only I can grasp happiness when it arrives
If only I can release my fear of vulnerability
The day I released my need to control
I finally stepped into my truth

I finally embraced my strength
I finally accepted happiness
All I have to do is be fully alive
Moment to moment

If Found, Please Return

I've lost something
Something invaluable to me
Without it I am nothing
Without I might as well cease to exist
Without it I am lost
If found, please return to me forthwith
Email me
Call me
Text me
Message me
Show up unannounced on my doorstep
I don't care
Just get it back to me
I need it
I'd do anything
I'd say anything
I'd give anything
For its safe return
Please, if you find
What I've lost
Bring it back to me
Give it back to me
Don't keep it from me
I beg of you
Return what I've lost
It's priceless to me
But likely of little use to you anyway
Oh, never mind
What am I saying?
You can't help
I learned long ago

Only I can find
What I've lost
When what I've lost
Is the most valuable thing I possess
The me that makes me… me

Refused and Released

You offered me so much
And yet I refused it
Not once
Not twice
But thrice
You scared me too much
You reached right through my defenses
And I couldn't have that
You melted the ice surrounding my heart
And doused the fire fortress I'd built
Nothing kept you out
Even when my feelings scorched you
Even when my words froze you
You smiled at me with your brilliance
I melted and cooled simultaneously
Fire and ice melded in perfect harmony
I wanted so much more of you
Than I could handle
So I did what I always do
When things get too intense
I pushed you away
I erected my ice wall
Surrounded by a fire wall
Convinced myself
If you breached one
The other would stop you
But hoped against hope
You'd break down my defenses
One last time, just one last time
So much for releasing you from my heart…

Exiting with Love

Don't think
Not even for a moment
My love for you
Makes me weak
I find more strength in love
Than in hate
Hate depletes me
Makes me feel less than I am
So while my heart is breaking
I love you still
I won't allow hate
To imprison me
In shackles
When I can break free with love
So I choose to love you
As I close the door and walk away
My heart argues with me
But I've spent too much of my life
Convincing others I'm worthy of them
It's time to stand up and say
See me for who I am
Or watch as I exit stage left
My heart sends you love
So that I can release you and me
So that I can free
Still, though closed
The door between us
Remains unlocked
Feel free to knock
I just might answer…

Question and Answer

I inhaled the question
My heart urged me to ignore
My brain pretended had no answer
My soul refused to hear
I let the question float through my body
It searched for acknowledgement
It needed a home
I fought the question
With every muscle
With every pore
With my very essence
Facing the question
Required I address my heart's desire
Urged me to apply my brain's logic
Forced my soul to consider my life
I fought the question with all my strength
Until, with body wrenching force,
I finally I exhaled the answer

You Do Not Know Me

You do not know me
You think you do
But you do not
How do I know?
You do not know me
Because you know only
What I want you to see
Or
Perhaps only what you choose to see
But either way
You do not know me
You think you do
You tell me who I am
You tell me who I should be
You tell me who I am not
You tell me who I shouldn't be
I used to listen and nod
I believed you
I thought you knew me
Better than I knew me
Then one day I realized
You do not know me
By then
I did not know me either
I took a deep sigh
Thought about all your
Declarations of who I was
And decided
I'm tired of trying to
Make you know me
So guess what

You'll just have to accept
You do not know me
And likely never really will

Knew My Heart

If you ever knew my heart
Really knew my heart
You would know I could never hate you
No matter what happened between us
Misdeeds and hurtful words
Blatant lies and truths
Misunderstandings and harmony
Secrets created and destroyed
Without even a moment to consider
The consequences our actions would create
I always thought you were the one who
Truly knew my heart with all its secret vulnerabilities
I thought I saw the truth of you
I thought I knew your heart
Really knew your heart
But perhaps it was all just fantasy
Two people seeing what they wanted to see
To make the moment work
Deluding ourselves to avoid reality
As I accept you're not the man I thought
And I'm better than the woman sought
I am left to wonder if you ever
Really knew my heart
But then the question arises
How could you have known my heart
Really known my heart
When I kept it hidden, even from myself

Redacted

Words spoken
Can never be redacted
Nor forgotten
They're etched on the heart
For all time
Left to remind us
How cruel we can be
When we speak thoughtless words
We can break a heart
Scars and stitches
Spoken in the language
Of emotion
What do we do when
Words that can't be redacted
Open old wounds
Breaking stitches
Bleeding all over our hearts
Spilling every last shard
Cutting into every
Attempt at forgiveness
I ache for soothing words
That will magically erase
The words
That cut so deeply
They become permanent fixtures
Changing my heart from open to closed…

Words: Love/Hate

Words
I love them
I hate them
They hold strength
They expose weakness
Words
I love them
I hate them
They bridge gaps
They expand crevices
Words
I love them
I hate them
They provide meaning
They erase truths
Words
I love them
I hate them
They change everything
They change nothing
Words
I love them
I hate them
They wield power
They steal strength
Words
I love them
I hate them
I can't live without them
I can't die because of them
Words

I love them
I hate them
They are the ultimate healers
They are the ultimate weapons
Words

Clutter

Clutter builds
Hiding in dusty corners
Burying the important underneath
Disguising the obvious
Stacks and stacks and stacks
Yesterday's needs hidden under today's wants
As I search for a way to clear the way for tomorrow
The clutter accumulates in the avoidance of loss
As I stare into the abyss of stuff that seemed so important
I just couldn't let go and yet I couldn't face
So I stacked it on top of one more stack
Stacks taking over the room
Holding the password to everything I am
Hidden in the clutter of the unimportant
Stacked so carefully to hide
The only thing that ever truly mattered
I clear away a stack
Wondering if another will take its place
Perhaps this time I'll be able to avoid the clutter
That comes with willful blindness
As the truth slaps the sight back into my eyes
In the clutter accumulated to hide my vulnerabilities
I reach for another stack avoiding the one that matters most
As I face the clutter one small step at a time
Realizing when I reach that final stack
I can no longer hide from what's left undone
Releasing the chaos
Hidden within the fortress of clutter
I've painstakingly built
What will I find when I finally
Clear the clutter

Blown Glass

Blown glass
Melting with heat
Stretching and bending
Melding into new shapes
Beautiful flaws accentuating intention
Air bubbles trapping you inside its structure
Hardening as it cools
A distinctive shape awaiting
Heat to meld it into something new
Perfection elusive in each unpredictable
Infusion of your breath and turn of the rod
Taking on a new form with each
Heating and cooling
If it doesn't work
Shatter it in with all the other
Abandoned pieces
Soon enough to be melted together
To recycle into something new
Unrecognizable from its origin

Taunts and Teases

Taunts and teases
The words ring through the air
Pointing out what sets me apart
Criticizing what you don't understand
Or what someone else told you was unacceptable
You don't reach out to make a connection
Schoolyard taunts from kindergarten
Grow crueler with each passing year
Until your words hit their target every time
Destroying any possibility of understanding
I turn on myself
Lobbing your
Teases and taunts
At myself
Before you load your ammunition
By the time your words hit
I'm already beaten down to the ground
You've succeeded
In convincing me I'm all you say I am
It won't be until years later
I'll ask myself
If your teases and taunts emanated from
Your own insecurities and home life
Or if you were just plain mean
Around the same time
I realize I let you treat me as somehow
Less than you
Because of my insecurities and home life
By then it will be too late for us to see
We could've been friends
If we'd sought to understand

Rather than exercise the age old
Divisive technique of
Taunts and teases

Compliments

"You're pure love"
"You're a gift"
"You are very sweet"
"You deserve to be happy"
I'm learning to accept
Such words spoken to me
When once I would've rejected them outright
Not me
I'm not pure love
I'm no one's gift
I don't do sweet
I don't deserve happiness
And yet
When I read these words today
From three different sources
I glowed
I tried them on for size
I smiled
I held them in my mind
I welcomed them into my heart
I whispered them on the wind
And my soul knew
They are true
I offer the world
My happiness
Sweetness
The gift of me
Pure love from my heart
It's all I have to offer
It's all any of us truly have to offer

Foundation

When people judge
As they will
Remember your foundation
It's where your strength lies
It's where your answers will find form

When people criticize
As they will
Remember your foundation
It's where your motivation solidifies
It's where your perseverance grows

When people betray
As they will
Remember your foundation
It's where your honesty begins
It's where your morality bolsters

When people leave
As they will
Remember your foundation
It's where your fortitude dwells
It's where your self stands

When people misunderstand
As they will
Remember your foundation
It's where your words find meaning
It's where your comprehension bridges

When people hate

As they will
Remember your foundation
It's where your love resides
It's where your worth glows

When people do what they will
As they will
Remember your foundation
It's where you begin and end
It's where you find all that matters

Foundation Fell Away

The foundation fell away
Why did I trust it?
Because I needed hope
Now it's nothing more than ash
Blowing away with each word spoken
Guess that's what I get
For allowing myself happiness

The Ledge

When you reach for someone you trust
And find no hand grasps yours
Leaving you dangling over the edge
Gripping a crumbling ledge with your fingertips
Wondering if you'll survive the fall
You know is coming
Heartache is compounded
You learn who needs released
You know where to not reach
Next time your heart cries

Left Side of the Bed

You left me
On the left side of the bed
My naked body pulsing
Awaiting discovery
Silently, begging for your touch
Refusing to speak the words aloud
My strength competed with my vulnerability
As I reached my left hand toward you
You turned back for a second
I imagined you returned to the bed
I so wanted to feel
Your intensity
Your arms around me
Your hands caress the curve of my hip
Your lips gently brush my cheek
I watched as you stood looking back
The expression on your face conflicted
Then I remembered
The left side of the bed belongs to you

Winter Forest

Walking through the winter forest
Bare branches crisscrossing above
Creating a lace patchwork quilt
Of sky and clouds
Sun peeking through
Warming the chill on my skin
Reminding me that I dressed to shield
The desolation from touching me
For in this winter landscape
Among the trees barren and strong
Leaves rotting atop dead grass
Lies everything we cherished
In those summer moments
When the greenery offered shade
From the burning sun
Shining down on our sweating skin
Bringing us to a frenzy
Memories bring a tear to my eye
Freezing in the winter cold
Salty icicles shattering on the ground
Snow floats past my heart
Through the barren branches
I look up longing for summer
For our summer
And trip over a fallen branch
Reminding me our summer is over
And sometimes winter lasts forever

Diamond

A lump of coal
Pressed and pressured
A gem retrieved
Cut and polished
An image cultivated
Artificial value assigned
True value hidden within
Raw and real
Bending to expectation
A brilliant smile
Created from
A million suppressed tears
Pressing down on
The lump of coal within
Creating a gem
Found worthy by
You

Don't

Don't lie to me
Don't tell me the truth
Don't push me
Don't need me
Don't neglect me
Don't rush me
Don't ask me
Don't stay
Don't leave
Don't hate me
Don't love me
All I ask is that you
Just
Don't
Not anymore
I can't take it if you
Do
I can't take it if you
Don't

Memories Chase Me

Hiding in myself
Withdrawing from you
My body closes on itself
Running from memories
That chase me without relent
Through woods
Up into the clouds
Over the mountains
Down to the sea's bottom
Across mountains
Through city streets
Memories I can never escape
Taking me back to the moment
And that other moment
No rescue came
Prayers went unanswered
My faith destroyed
My trust evaporated
My naiveté demolished
My confidence beaten bloody
Leaving me to know
Only I can save me
Counting on a white knight
Only leads to my demise
So as the memories chase me
From year to year
From place to place
From reality to reality
From fantasy to fantasy
All I can do is remind myself
I survived the event

And the other one, too
I will survive the memories
As I have year after year
In place after place
Living reality after reality
Hiding in fantasy after fantasy
Yet, I still feel myself
Spiraling down, down, down
To a place I don't want to go
As least now I know
As the memories recede
Like the tides
I will once again thrive
Traveling up, up, up
As the memories chase me

Cradle My Heart

Cradle my heart
With your good intentions
Show me a path I'd never take
Lift me above the clouds to watch
The stars discover the inky night
Run your hands over my scars
Feel each experience come to life
In memories I can never leave
The truth of who I was
Vibrating through who I've become
Asking if you can see beyond who you knew
To discover the me life has created
As I offer you a battered heart
Ready to heal
In a cradle of love

Intuition

My heart says you need me
My brain says I have to be smart
So I sit quietly
Allowing them to argue
Wondering does intuition
Come from the heart
Or the brain
For today in this struggle
It seems intuition is lost
Confusion has taken over
My heart says you love me
My brain says your kind of love hurts
As the battle rages between the two
I question my instincts
As I long to reach out to you
Are you worth the risk?
My heart makes excuses
My brain reminds me of every misdeed
As they fight to the death
Each confident in their chosen stance
I sit quietly
Feeling that space between the two
That says
They're both right
The question is
Do I take the chance?
Follow my intuition with reservations
Or let go of any possibility of us…

Mustang

You attempted to break me
Like a wild Mustang
Caught in the mountains
Removed from its home
Separated from its family
Corralled me
Forced the bit in my mouth
Pulled the bridle over my ears
I shook my head, snorted, pulled away
When my fight died down
The fear in my eyes all that was left
You patted my neck, smoothed back my mane
Placed your hand over my heart
Listening to my heavy breathing
You walked me around and around that corral
Pulling this way and that with the reigns
The bit pulling in my mouth
Next came the saddle
You tossed a blanket over my back
Waited for me to fight it
Walked me with only the blanket
Why you wanted this of me I didn't understand
I shook it off
I stomped my foot
I protested
Finally I accepted
Then you placed the saddle over the blanket
The weight uncomfortable, unknown
I stomped my feet
I shook my head
I snorted

The fear in my eyes never dying
You whispered for me to trust you
How could I?
You took me from everything I loved
You penned me in
You bridled me
As you tightened the girth
I feared the saddle would never leave me
I bucked and reared trying to shake it off
You told me to calm down, to trust you
All I wanted was to roam free
To return to all I loved
Yet you insisted I serve your needs
You walked me around the paddock
Dressed in my bridle and saddle
I calmed down thinking if I pleased you
You'd release me
Instead, you had other plans
You put your foot in the stirrup
Slung your leg over me
Settled into that saddle
I panicked
You had no right to be on my back
Yet there you were
I bucked, I reared, I ran
You held on tight
Assuring you me you wouldn't hurt me
Never recognizing the distress I felt
As you attempted to break me
My spirit went dormant
Awaited the day I could once again run free
Just like a broken Mustang's

Impress Me

I'm not impressed
That
You can
Down a fifth of whiskey
Or drink a six-pack in one sitting
Or eat a twenty ounce porterhouse
Or kill a deer with a large rack
Or catch the biggest fish in the pond
Or beat up the guy who hit on me
Or curse louder than the next guy
Or flex biceps as large as my thigh
Or whistle at me as I walk past
Or tell the crudest joke
Or drive the fastest car
Or charm me with smooth words
Or deceive me without guilt
No, none of that is impressive
In fact, it's a huge turn-off
What impresses me
Is
When your kindness shines
When you gently hold the tiniest kitten in your palm
Or softly pet the smallest puppy
Or listen to a child's story with rapt attention
Or hold my hand when my heart is breaking
Or dry my tears from my cheeks without a word
Or listen, really listen, to my truth
Or cook me a special meal
Or remember my favorite dark chocolate
Or try a new lifestyle with me
Or refuse to hurt an animal

Or hug me for no reason
Or smile when you see me enter a room
Or make me laugh when my heart aches
Or offer to help someone in need
Or speak the truth when a lie would be easier
Or cry when your heart aches with loss
So if you want to impress me
Don't set out to prove how macho you are
Show me how caring you are
Show me you're human
Show me what makes you vulnerable
Then I'll see your true strength
Tough doesn't impress me
Be strong enough to be weak with me
Then I'll finally be impressed…

Our Times

Your hand slides across the table
Inching toward mine
As your fingers touch mine
You look up to search my face for my reaction
I look down into my glass of water
Hoping you won't see me catch my breath
Hoping you won't notice the chill spread over my skin
Hoping you won't feel my pulse quicken
We've been here time and again
Always searching for the right moment to connect
Never finding it
Teasing each other with possibilities
Recognizing all our talk is little more than fantasy
You intertwine your fingers in mine
A tear threatens to roll down my cheek
After all our mistakes can we breech those barricades
To allow our vulnerabilities to draw us closer
Or will we walk to the edge of paradise
Only to run in opposite directions as soon as we get too close
I look up into your eyes
Your eyes say what your lips can't
You feel the connection, too
It's never truly left
No matter what we've tried
Distorted, contorted, bent, corroded, frayed, collapsed
This connection between us has suffered severe damage
And yet it remains
So if you're going to make that move and grasp my hand
Be prepared
This woman no longer runs away when things get too intense
If it's time for us to move from fantasy to reality

Then we have to make this our time
No hesitation, no fear, no holding back
No clock ticking down the minutes until we say goodbye
Time won't wait for us to make our connection
If you want it, my hand lies on the table for the grasping
Waiting, hoping, longing, anticipating…

Pleasure's Touch

Quietly you came
Quietly you left
First you touched me
Your hands offering me beauty
In a gentle caress that lingers
Against my skin still
Your lips offering me beauty
In an urgent brush that lingers
On my lips still
You touched me slowly
Frighteningly slowly
Each move deliberate, exciting, exploratory
Almost as if you intended to memorize
Every inch of me
Your touch urged me toward lost control
Your touch quickened in rhythm
As my body arched for you
I felt you like a dream
Slide over my body
Taking me to paradise
You gazed into my eyes
Passion, desire, love
Brought us to ecstasy
As the moon shined upon
Our bare vulnerabilities
Leaving us open to
Pleasure's touch

Handed

I handed you me
I don't know why
Before you came along
I handled me just fine
But you
Patted my head
Held my hand
Scolded me
Offered to take over
Wanted to fix me
For some reason
I decided you knew better
How I should be
So when I grew weary of fighting
I handed you me
Now I look at me and see
Exactly what I never wanted to be
I look at you and find
Someone who never really knew me
Leaving me sad that
I handed you me
Sorry, but I've decided
To take me back
I'm sure I can do better than
How you handled me
After
I handed you me

Please

Take me in your arms, please
Hold me while I release you, please
Understand I can't forget you, please
Love me through the end, please
Accept my love as real, please
Remind me this is as it must be, please
Lie to me, just this once, please
Promise me tomorrow, please
Find me when you need me, please
Know I'll always adore you, please
Give me a little space to find my place, please
Let me know you're okay, or not, please
Stay in touch, please
Feel my love when your heart hurts, please
Reach for me when memories bombard you, please
Come see me, please
Miss me on occasion, please
Look for me in quiet moments, please
Remember me with fondness, please
Smile when you think of me, please
May I do the same, please?

Hold Through This

I will hold you through this
But who will hold me
Staring into your eyes
Your pain on display
Mine screaming inside my heart
You slide your arms around me
Tell me you'll
Hold me through this
But how can you
When you're the cause of this
You take responsibility
It's not enough
Your concern I'll self-destruct
Bleeds into your words, actions
Leaving me strangely defensive
Wondering why you think
You still have that much power
I will keep your secret
I will protect you as best I can
I will love you
But I love myself far too much
To risk my destruction
I know that may sound strange
But the truth is
I will hold me through this
I will hold you through this
I will even allow you to hold me
I will take the comfort you offer
Because I need it right now
But I won't promise your arms
Will be my safe place any longer

And someday I will find
Someone who holds me through my pain
Just as I held you through yours

Rescue

I never asked you to rescue me
I never needed rescued
Regardless of what you thought
At least, not the way you thought
You looked in my face and saw pain
You looked in my eyes and saw fear
You looked in my heart and saw uncertainty
You wanted to take it all away
You wanted to guard me from the memories
You wanted to take away the experience
That was never your job
All I wanted was for you to
Walk beside me
Hold my hand
Share new experiences, good experiences
Seeing the survivor in me
Who was stronger than the victim in me
See, while I may have wanted someone else to save me
On some level I always knew
Only I could save me
So the harder you tried
The more I withdrew into myself
You needed the victory over my demons
Even it was a false triumph
You still think you saved me from myself
While I know the truth
Only I can release me from my demons

Conformity

Free to fly
Above the clouds
Looking down at
All I'm leaving behind
Knowing my liberation from expectation
Comes with a high price
Leaving behind convention
So I can embrace the woman I am
Grasping a guide rope
Cutting loose the anchor
Denying your tether to me
As I strive to feel the strength inside
To tell you
This is me
You can like me as I am
Or you can leave
But you do not get to force
Me to conform to your whims
Love me for all of me
The naughty and the nice
Or close the door behind you
On your way out of my life

Vulnerability in Silhouette

I guarded my vulnerability like a rare gem
Pushed it into a vault where it couldn't sparkle
Killed the possibility of it giving me strength
I saw vulnerability as my enemy
An enemy I needed to imprison
Terrified it would reveal my secrets
Give those who'd needed it ammunition
To wreak havoc on my carefully constructed image
While destroying the core I hid behind a fortress of bravado
So I held my head high
Put on a mask of strength
Hid my fear behind a welcoming smile
Walked a determined stride
Never slowed my pace
Reaching for the farthest goal
The one I knew impossible to reach
Promised myself no one would ever touch that place
The place where
My vulnerability became a mere silhouette

ACKNOWLEDGMENTS

Loay Abu-Husein earned my appreciation by working tirelessly with me to create a cover that expresses my vision for this book. I'm also grateful for his ongoing love and support.

Cynthia "Ariel" Evans, Joanne Pence, Lori Felmey, Kenisha Henning, and Kaylee Truesdell provided thoughtful and helpful feedback on the cover. I feel so grateful for their input, support, and encouragement!

I continue to be grateful to myriad poets for feedback on individual poems in this collection. Ariel, Tony Haynes, Heather Parker, Butch Knight, and Joshua Timothy Simms all offered feedback, encouragement, and inspiration as did many other members of the Facebook groups, *Poet* and *Spiritual Poems*.

I also offer my gratitude to the many family members, friends, and fans who continue to read and appreciate my work.

PRAISE FOR T. L. COOPER'S BOOKS

Soaring Betrayal

"…I found myself unable to put down the book, but kept reading from one story to the next… - Lucy

Strength in Silhouette

"…Often harsh in its realism, it also can soar with delicate and unexpected nuance…" - Lucy

Memory in Silhouette

"…pithy examination of relational memories should help every poet discover an inner part of their own memories. I highly recommend this poetic study in life lived and memories examined." – Auburn McCanta, author of All the Dancing Birds

Reflections in Silhouette:

"…Brave enough to lower the curtain into her own heart, T.L. gives the reader that certain leverage where one might be able to find the strength, upon reflection, to go forward into the bright sunshine of their own new day…" - Ray Ellis, author of the Nate Richards Series.

Love in Silhouette:

"…Love in Silhouette" is a delightfully honest and open-faced collection of poetry that leaves you feeling as though you have peeked in on intimate moments of the author's love life…" - Mary Braun, co-author of Opposites Attract: A Haiku Tete-a-Tete.

All She Ever Wanted:

"...A thoughtful, insightful look into the changing human mind and spirit evoked by an interracial friendship, All She Ever Wanted is a superbly written, highly recommended novel showcasing a theme that is as historic and universal as interracial human experience, and contemporary as today's newspaper headlines..." - Midwest Book Review.

ABOUT THE AUTHOR

T. L. Cooper is an author and poet whose work aims to empower and inspire through an exploration of the human condition. Her poems, short stories, articles, and essays have appeared online, in books, and in magazines. Her published books include a collection of short stories, *Soaring Betrayal*, her *Silhouette Poetry Series*, and a novel, *All She Ever Wanted*. She grew up on a farm in Tollesboro, Kentucky. When not writing, she enjoys yoga, golf, hiking, and traveling. She currently lives in Albany, Oregon with her husband and three cats.

www.ingramcontent.com/pod-product-compliance
Lightning Source LLC
Chambersburg PA
CBHW051806040426
42446CB00007B/535